AMERICA
the Beautiful

Going-to-the-Sun Mountain, Glacier National Park, Montana

AMERICA
the Beautiful

COURAGE
BOOKS
AN IMPRINT OF RUNNING PRESS
PHILADELPHIA · LONDON

9   8   7   6   5   4   3   2   1
Digit on the right indicates the number of this printing

Library of Congress Control Number: 2004110026

ISBN 0-7624-2355–2

Cover and interior design by Corinda Cook
Photo research by Susan Oyama
Edited by Jennifer Leczkowski
Typography: Baskerville, Caslon, GillSans, Minion,
Poppl-Residenz, and Trajan

This book may be ordered by mail from the publisher.
But try your bookstore first!

Published by Courage Books, an imprint of
Running Press Book Publishers
125 South Twenty-second Street
Philadelphia, Pennsylvania 19103-4399

Visit us on the web!
www.runningpress.com

Front cover: Trout Lake area, San Juan Mountains, Colorado

Back cover: El Capitan, Yosemite National Park, California

Back flap: Mt. Clement, Montana

CONTENTS

AMERICA
the Beautiful

Inspired by the classic poem "America the Beautiful," written by Katharine Lee Bates in 1893, this book is a glorious collection of Bates's beloved verse, inspirational quotations, and stirring images, brilliantly depicting the history, diversity, and spirit of America.

"America the Beautiful" is the result of an exhilarating lecture trip to the top of Pikes Peak in Colorado, where Katharine Lee Bates, a poet and pioneering young English professor from Wellesley College, was awe-struck by the breathtaking panorama she beheld atop that mountain: "It was then and there," she wrote, "as I was looking out over the sea-like expanse of fertile country spreading away so far under those ample skies, that the opening lines of the hymn floated into my mind."

Her poem was first published on July 4, 1895 in the weekly newspaper *The Congregationalist*—for which Bates was paid $5—and was revised and reprinted in 1904 for *The Boston Evening Transcript*, and again in 1913. Although never originally intended to be sung, the poem's fine sense of patriotism caused it to be set to at least 74 different melodies, including "Auld Lang Syne."

Today, Bates's poem is voiced to the hymn "Materna," composed in 1882 by church organist and choirmaster Samuel A. Ward—nearly a decade before the poem was written. The writer and composer never met, but their works are forever united in the celebrated song that, though never made "official," remains a favorite national anthem along "The Star Spangled Banner"—defining the beauty and optimism of America.

North Gateway Rock and Pikes Peak,
Garden of the Gods, Colorado Springs, Colorado

AMERICA *the Beautiful*

O beautiful for spacious skies,
For amber waves of grain,
For purple mountain majesties
Above the fruited plain!
America! America!
God shed His grace on thee
And crown thy good with brotherhood
From sea to shining sea!

O beautiful for pilgrim feet
Whose stern, impassioned stress
A thoroughfare for freedom beat
Across the wilderness!
America! America!
God mend thine every flaw,
Confirm thy soul in self-control,
Thy liberty in law!

O beautiful for heroes proved
In liberating strife
Who more than self their country loved
And mercy more than life!
America! America!
May God thy gold refine
Til all success be nobleness
And every gain divine!

O beautiful for patriot dream
That sees beyond the years
Thine alabaster cities gleam
Undimmed by human tears!
America! America!
God shed His grace on thee
And crown thy good with brotherhood
From sea to shining sea!

NATURAL
Treasures

The whole landscape showed design,
like man's noblest sculptures.
How wonderful the power of its beauty! . . .
Beauty beyond thought everywhere,
beneath, above, made, and being made forever.

—John Muir
(1838–1914)
American naturalist

Turet Arch through North Window,
Arches National Park, Utah

Mt. Katahdin and Sandy Stream Pond, Baxter State Park, Maine

Did you ever see a place that looks like it was
built just to enjoy? Well, this whole state of
Maine looks that way. If it's not a beautiful lake,
it's a beautiful tree, or a pretty green
hay meadow. And beautiful old-time houses,
with barns built right in with the kitchens.

—Will Rogers
(1879–1935)
American humorist and actor

17

THERE IS NOT

A SPRIG OF GRASS

THAT SHOOTS

UNINTERESTING TO ME.

–Thomas Jefferson
(1743–1826)
American president

Grasses on
Algonquin Peak,
Adirondack
Park and Forest
Preserve, New York

For this is what America is about.
It is the uncrossed desert
and the unclimbed ridge.
It is the star that is not reached
and the harvest that is
sleeping in the unplowed ground.

—Lyndon B. Johnson
(1908–1973)
American president

The Mojave is a big desert and a frightening one.
It's as though nature tested a man
for endurance and constancy to prove whether
he was good enough to get to California.

–John Steinbeck
(1902–1968)
American author

Joshua Tree,
Joshua Tree National
Park, California

Whatever events in progress shall disgust men with cities, and infuse

them into the passion for country life, and country pleasures,

will render a service to the whole face of this continent, and will

further the most poetic of all the occupations of real life,

the bringing out by art the native but hidden graces of the landscape.

—Ralph Waldo Emerson
(1803–1882)
American essayist and poet

Glade Creek Mill,
Babcock State Park,
West Virginia

Frosted sand dunes, Monument Valley Tribal Park, Arizona

All the aspects of this desert are beautiful,

whether you behold it in fair weather or foul,

or when the sun is just breaking out after a storm,

and shining on its moist surface in the distance,

it is so white, and pure, and level, and each slight

inequality and rack is so distinctly revealed;

and when your eyes slide off this, they fall on the ocean.

—Henry David Thoreau
(1817–1862)
American author and naturalist

America does not concern itself now with Impressionism. We own no involved philosophy. The psyche of the land is to be found in its movement. It is to be felt as a dramatic force of energy and vitality.

–Martha Graham
(1894–1991)
American dancer and choreographer

Vernal Falls,
Yosemite National
Park, California

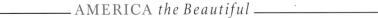

When I think of death, I only regret that I will not be able to see

this beautiful country anymore . . .

unless the Indians are right and my spirit will walk here after I'm gone.

—Georgia O'Keeffe
(1887–1986)
American painter

Anasazi Cliff Dwelling, Arizona

Redwood National Park, California

THE FORESTS OF AMERICA,
HOWEVER SLIGHTED BY MAN,
MUST HAVE BEEN A GREAT
DELIGHT TO GOD, BECAUSE THEY
WERE THE BEST HE EVER PLANTED.

–John Muir
(1838–1914)
American naturalist

I see an America

whose rivers and valleys and lakes,

hills and streams and plains;

the mountains over our land and

nature's wealth deep under the earth,

are protected as the rightful heritage of all the people.

–Franklin D. Roosevelt
(1882–1945)
American president

Grand Teton National Park, Wyoming

The East is a montage . . .

It is old and it is young, very green in summer,

very white in winter, gregarious, withdrawn,

and at once both sophisticated and provincial.

—Phyllis McGinley
(1905–1978)
American writer

Red Pine forest,
Quabbin Reservation,
Massachusetts

God bless America, land that I love,

Stand beside her, and guide her,

Through the night, with the light from above,

From the mountains, to the prairies

To the oceans, white with foam

God bless America, my home sweet home,

God bless America! My Home Sweet Home!

–Irving Berlin
(1888–1989)
American composer and lyricist

Heceta Head
Lighthouse, Oregon

COMMUNITY
and Strength

Colorful cottages, Bayside, Northport, Maine

Farmland, Lancaster County, Pennsylvania

AMERICA IS NOT A BLANKET WOVEN FROM ONE THREAD, ONE COLOR, ONE CLOTH.

—Jesse Jackson
(b. 1941)
American politician and activist

. . . America is a family . . .
We've got to start
remembering that no member
of our family should
be satisfied if any member of
our American family is
suffering or in need and
we can do something about it.

–Colin Powell
(b. 1937)
American Secretary of State

Intellectually I know that America is no better than any other country; emotionally I know she is better than every other country.

–Sinclair Lewis
(1885–1951)
American writer

Then join hands, brave America all, by uniting we stand, by dividing we fall.

—John Dickinson
(1732–1808)
American patriot and statesman

Midtown, New York City, New York

NO MATTER HOW HARD THE LOSS,

DEFEAT MIGHT SERVE AS WELL

AS VICTORY TO SHAKE THE SOUL

AND LET THE GLORY OUT.

—Al Gore
  (b. 1948)
  American vice president

Lupines and
White Mountains,
Sugar Hill,
New Hampshire

He who believes is strong; he who doubts is weak.

Strong convictions precede great actions.

–Louisa May Alcott
(1832–1888)
American author

Devil's Tower, Devil's Tower National Monument, Wyoming

Independence Hall,
Philadelphia, Pennsylvania

Four score and seven years ago
our fathers brought forth
on this continent a new nation,
conceived in liberty,
and dedicated to the proposition
that all men are created equal.

–Abraham Lincoln
(1809–1865)
American president

. . . established upon those principles of freedom, equality, justice, and humanity
for which American patriots sacrificed their lives and fortunes.
I therefore believe it is my duty to my country to love it, to support its constitution,
to obey its laws, to respect its flag, and to defend it against all enemies.

–William Tyler Page
(1811–1885)
American artist

I see America,

not in the setting sun of a black night of despair ahead of us,

I see America in the crimson light of a rising sun fresh from the burning,

creative hand of God. I see great days ahead,

great days possible to men and women of will and vision . . .

—Carl Sandburg
(1878–1967)
American poet

Great Smoky Mountains National Park, North Carolina

Rooftops near Peekskill, New York

Let every man honor and love
the land of his birth and the race from
which he springs and keep their memory green.
It is a pious and honorable duty.
But let us have done with British-Americans
and Irish-Americans and German-Americans,
and so on, and all be Americans.

—Henry Cabot Lodge
(1850–1924)
American politician and writer

America has never been united by blood or birth or soil. We are bound by ideals that

move us beyond our backgrounds, lift us above our interests and teach us what it means

to be citizens. Every child must be taught these principles. Every citizen must uphold them.

And every immigrant, by embracing these ideals, makes our country more, not less, American.

–George W. Bush
(b. 1946)
American president

Our nation is a mansion erected on three powerful pillars:
the creative mix of our citizens;
the moral, political, and economic principles
which it built; and, basic to all else,
the glorious land we have been able to occupy.

–James A. Michener
(b. 1907)
American writer

United States Capitol,
Washington, D.C.

INHABITING
the Land

North Platte River Valley farmland,
between Ogallala and Lewellen, Nebraska

... in western Nebraska,
fields give way to the great cattle
ranches of the sandhill area,
life is more leisurely, and manners
are more relaxed. Something
of the Old West still survives.

–Federal Writers Project

... it is the inexhaustible land of wheat, maize, wool, flax, coal, iron, beef and pork, butter and cheese, apples and grapes—and of ten million virgin farms— to the eye at present wild and unproductive—yet experts say that upon it when irrigated may easily be grown enough wheat to feed the world.

—Walt Whitman
(1819–1892)
American poet

It is not unkind to say,

from the standpoint

of scenery alone, that if

many, and indeed most,

of our American national

parks were to be set

down on the continent

of Europe thousands of

Americans would journey

all the way across

the ocean in order to

see their beauties.

–Franklin D. Roosevelt
  (1882–1945)
  American president

Yellowstone National Park, Wyoming

Skyline, Seattle, Washington

I look forward to an America which will not be afraid of grace and beauty,
which will protect the beauty of our natural environment, which will
preserve the great old American houses and squares and parks of our national
past and which will build handsome and balanced cities for our future.

–John F. Kennedy
(1917–1963)
American president

The bridges—and heaven knows Seattle
has them—wear necklaces of light,
which they reflect on the dark waters.

—Harry Lee Jones
(1921–1983)
American writer

IOWA, LUSHLY FERTILE, AGRISTRATE EXTRAORDINARY, LANDLOCKED, AMERICAN GOTHIC, BIRTHPLACE OF HERBERT HOOVER AND HENRY WALLACE, HOME OF THE FORMER'S PRESIDENTIAL LIBRARY, IS THE QUINTESSENCE OF AMERICA.

–Neal R. Peirce
Twentieth-century American writer

The fields have turned, yellow and light brown;
central Iowa gets most of its autumn from the fields.
Trees and brush trim the roadsides and fence rows vividly,
but the great reaching planes of quiet colors are the fields.

–Hamlin Garlin
(1860–1940)
American writer

Farm and hay bales, Winneshiek County, Iowa

Mississippi River at North Marquette Access, Iowa

Mississippi begins in the lobby of a Memphis, Tennessee, hotel and extends south to the Gulf of Mexico. It is dotted with little towns concentric about the ghosts of the horses and mules once tethered to the hitchrail enclosing the county courthouse . . .

—William Faulkner
  (1897–1962)
  American writer

As one comes down the Henry Hudson Parkway along the river in the dusk,
New York is never real; it is always fabulous.

—Anthony Bailey
(b. 1933)
English writer

George Washington Bridge
and New York City skyline, New York

... Alaska, for all of us ...
was synonymous with the gold and glamour
of the Yukon and Klondike:
the home of sourdoughs and Eskimos ...

–Dwight D. Eisenhower
(1890–1969)
American president

Icebergs, Stikine-LeConte Wilderness,
Tongass National Forest, Alaska

The attraction and superiority of California are in its days. It has better days, and more of them, than any other country.

—Ralph Waldo Emerson
(1803–1882)
American essayist and poet

Tip the world over on its side and everything loose will land in Los Angeles.

–Frank Lloyd Wright
(1869–1959)
American architect

Pacific Ocean
coastline,
California

FREEDOM
to Dream

Statue of Liberty, Liberty Island, New York

The future belongs to those who believe in the beauty of their dreams.

—Eleanor Roosevelt
(1884–1962)
American first lady and humanitarian

THAT'S ONE SMALL STEP FOR A MAN,
ONE GIANT LEAP FOR MANKIND.

–Neil Armstrong
(b. 1930)
American astronaut

Golden Gate Bridge,
San Francisco, California

We stand today on the edge of a new frontier.

–John F. Kennedy
(1917–1963)
American president

Books were my pass to personal freedom.
I learned to read at age three, and soon
discovered there was a whole world to conquer
that went beyond our farm in Mississippi.

—Oprah Winfrey
(b. 1954)
American television personality and actress

Morro Bay environs,
California

America is a land of wonders,
in which everything is in
constant motion and every change
seems an improvement.

—Alexis de Tocqueville
(1805–1859)
French politician and writer

Michigan Avenue,
Chicago, Illinois

Canola fields, Palouse Hills, Washington

Liberty, when it begins to take root, is a plant of rapid growth.

—George Washington
(1732–1799)
American president

Now, I say to you today my friends, even though we face the difficulties of today and tomorrow, I still have a dream. It is a dream deeply rooted in the American dream …

—Martin Luther King, Jr.
(1929–1968)
American civil rights leader

Freedom is not something that anybody can be given.
Freedom is something people take,
and people are as free as they want to be.

—James Baldwin
(1924–1987)
American writer

Mount Rushmore National Memorial, South Dakota

Geese flying south near Whitehorse,
Lancaster County, Pennsylvania

Never give in and never give up.

—Hubert H. Humphrey
(1911–1978)
American vice president

The work goes on, the cause endures, the hope still lives, and the dreams shall never die.

–Senator Edward Kennedy
(b. 1932)
American senator

And the sea will grant each man new hope . . .
his sleep brings dreams of home.

—Christopher Columbus
(1451–1506)
Italian explorer

Big Sur,
California

Sandy Hook, New Jersey

Liberty must at all hazards be supported.

We have a right to it, derived from our Maker.

But if we had not, our fathers have earned

and bought it for us, at the expense of their ease,

their estates, their pleasure, and their blood.

–John Adams
  (1735–1826)
  American president

Without Freedom of Thought there can be no such Thing as Wisdom; and no such Thing as Public Liberty, without Freedom of Speech.

—Benjamin Franklin
  (1706–1790)
  American statesman, scientist, and philosopher

THERE IS A CERTAIN
ENTHUSIASM IN LIBERTY
THAT MAKES HUMAN
NATURE RISE ABOVE
ITSELF, IN ACTS OF
BRAVERY AND HEROISM.

–Alexander Hamilton
(1755–1804)
American statesman

Children should be educated and instructed
in the principles of freedom.

–John Adams
(1735–1826)
American president

United States Marine
Corps War Memorial,
Arlington, Virginia

America . . . It is a fabulous country, the only fabulous country; it is the only place where miracles not only happen, but where they happen all the time.

–Thomas Wolfe
(1900–1938)
American writer

Rainbow, Denali
National Park
and Preserve, Alaska

PHOTOGRAPHY *Credits*